D1774055

FRUSTRATED

by Penny Anderson
illustrated by
Dan Siculan

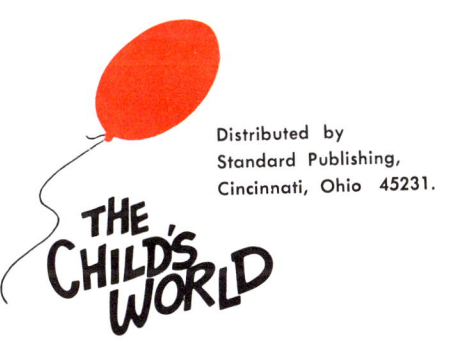

Distributed by
Standard Publishing,
Cincinnati, Ohio 45231.

ELGIN, ILLINOIS 60120

Note to parents and teachers:

Feelings are genuine responses to life situations. Sometimes our feelings are appropriate to those situations. Sometimes they are not. Regardless, we need to accept our feelings, and direct expressions of feeling positively if we hope to be effective Christian witnesses.

The feelings of children are intense. There is beauty in that. And there is promise. But in the expression of feeling, problems sometimes arise. Uncontrolled or misdirected expression of negative feeling can be harmful.

This book presents a number of situations that can cause frustration. Use these situations to promote discussion. Help children identify positive outlets for their frustration in actions that will help, rather than harm, themselves and others.

Most situations in which we find ourselves contain humor. Sometimes children see that best.

Distributed by Standard Publishing, 8121 Hamilton Avenue, Cincinnati, Ohio 45231

Library of Congress Cataloging in Publication Data
Anderson, Penny S.
  Frustrated.

  (What does it mean?)
  Summary: Describes a number of situations which can cause frustration, such as breaking and losing items, staying inside on a rainy day, being called names, and feeling sick.
  1. Frustration—Juvenile literature.
[1. Frustration]   I. Siculan, Dan, ill.
II. Title.   III. Series.
BF575.F7A57   152.4   82-4492
ISBN 0-89565-237-4   AACR2

© 1982 The Child's World, Inc.
All rights reserved. Printed in U.S.A.

FRUSTRATED

Jesus said, "Take heart!
I have overcome the world!"
—John 16:33b [NIV]

Today was such a bad day, Lord!
   My music box
   crashed to the floor
   when I bumped it.
   The lady's head broke off.

All day long, things went wrong.
   A ball hit me
   right in the face.
   My shoelace came untied—
   and I tripped on it.

There's a trying-not-to-cry
   hurt in my throat, Lord.
   What did you do
   when you had a bad day?

       —Sylvia Root Tester

When accidents happen,
I GET FRUSTRATED

"Let me pour it . . .
I can do it!"
"You may try," she said.

When I poured,
of course, I spilled it
all over Jamie's head.

Mr. Northrup raises roses—
pink and yellow, white and red.
All the dirt is soft around them,
a warm and fragrant
flower bed.

Mr. Northrup watched me riding
my new, blue, two-wheeled bike.
I waved at him and ran right over
those bright roses
we both like.

All the branches and the petals
splattered, shattered in the dirt.
They were ruined, but Mr. Northrup
ran to see
if I was hurt.

I wasn't hurt. I was frustrated.
I wanted to run away and hide.
It seems as if I do something stupid
every time
I ride.

Then there are things
I just can't do and—
I AM FRUSTRATED

"Don't hold it like that.
Choke up on the bat!
Spread your feet apart.
Shape up! Look smart!"

I can't EVER do
what they tell me to—
keep my eye on the ball,
swing hard and not fall!

"Emily Ann's a scaredy-cat.
Emily Ann's afraid...."

I climbed it once
and fell on my head.
I skinned my knee;
it even bled.

"Emily Ann's a scaredy-cat.
Emily Ann's afraid...."
   I'll climb it again
   and probably fall—
   or maybe pretend
   I don't hear them call.

"Emily Ann's a scaredy-cat.
Emily Ann's afraid...."
   Don't call me names;
   you never should.
   It frustrates me
   and I don't feel good.

   Besides, I am NOT a scaredy-cat!
   I am NOT afraid!

A hungry grey squirrel
   with a fluffy, puffy tail
   sat on our fence.
   His paws were folded
   like praying hands
across his furry chest.

I tried to paint
   a picture of him.
   I worked all during snacks
   while Timmy stuffed crackers
   in his mouth
and laughed at my mistakes.

When things go wrong,

I FEEL FRUSTRATED

Daddy said he'd take me fishing.
    He promised me we'd go
Down along the river bank
    Where the cattails grow.

Mommy said that Daddy called.
    He has to work tonight.
There's nothing to do but sit around,
    Pretending it's all right.

When I ate my soup,
   I burned my tongue.
I pinched my finger
   in the dresser drawer.
My left shoe's tied
   with the tongue outside,
and my right one
   walks all wrong.

Where is it?
   Where is it?

Where's my chocolate rabbit
I saved here in my drawer?

It's gone!
   All gone!

I saved it to take for show and tell
And to eat at recess.

Where did it go, Jeff?
   Where did it go?

YOU
   ATE
      IT?
         NO!

It's raining,
    It's raining,
        It's raining again.

Won't it ever stop?
Katy wants to go with me
To play on the swings
In the park.
But . . .

It's raining,
    It's raining,
        It's raining again.

It's raining everywhere,
So Katy can't come play with me.
And I can't play
With her.

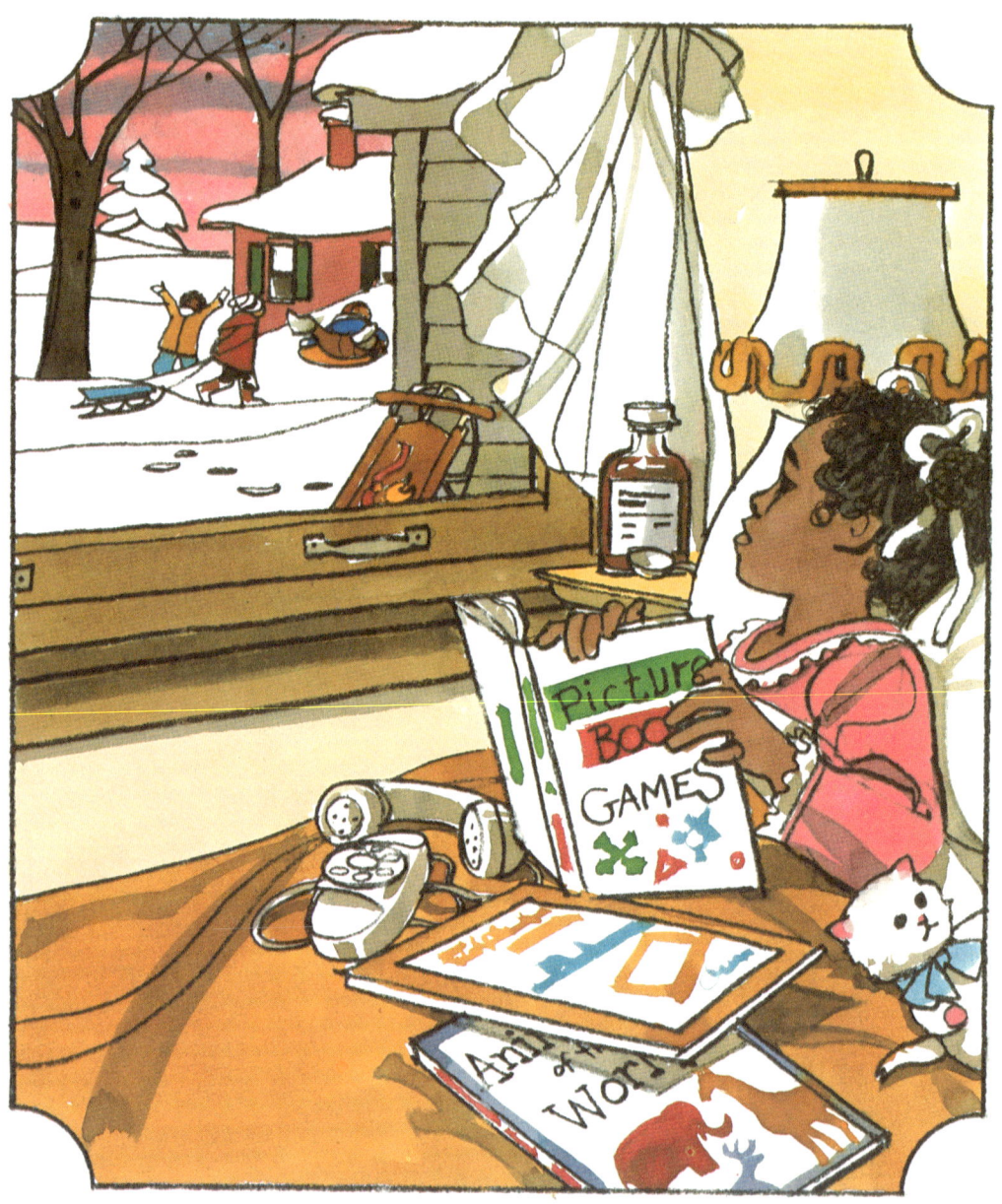

I want to go out and play in the snow—
   Slide down the hill on my sled.
But I can't play out and run and shout.
   I have to stay in bed.

My blanket's too hot. My pillows are flat.
   My puzzle fell on the floor.
My head aches, my eyes hurt,
   And my throat is getting sore.

But I want to go out and play in the snow—
   Slide down the hill on my sled.
I want to play out and run and shout.
   I don't want to stay in bed.

And too many don'ts make me
FRUSTRATED

Don't run,
WALK!

Don't yell,
TALK!

Don't spill,
DRINK!

Don't forget,
THINK!

Don't smash,
FIX!

Don't bite,
KISS!

Don't hate,
LOVE!

Too many don'ts make me
FRUSTRATED!

Dear God,

I have some bad days
when everything goes wrong.
On those days
I act mad, sad, or bad.
I can't be good
all the time.
Nobody can.

I'll bet you understand
when I'm frustrated
and nothing is going right
for me. Help everyone else
to understand, too!
Help them to know
I really care, and that
I love You.

       Amen.

About the Author:

Penny Anderson holds a degree in elementary education from Western Illinois University. A former Illinois State University faculty associate who taught language arts in the Metcalf Laboratory School, Ms. Anderson has written extensively for teachers—and for children. She and her husband now live in New Smyrna Beach, Florida.

About the Artist:

Dan Siculan studied art fundamentals at the Oglebay Institute in Wheeling, West Virginia, and life drawing at the American Academy of Art in Chicago. His career began while in the army where he served as an artist while stationed in Europe. Mr. Siculan later worked as a commercial artist, becoming free lance in 1951. He is proficient in painting in oils, acrylics, and water color media and has produced numerous editions of original serigraphs. He is married and has four children and three grandchildren.